SUCCESSFUL GARDENING IN UTAH

Caleb Warnock

 THE BACKYARD RENAISSANCE COLLECTION

DISCOVER THE LONG-LOST SKILLS OF SELF-RELIANCE

My name is Caleb Warnock, and I've been working for years to learn how to return to forgotten skills, the skills of our ancestors. As our world becomes increasingly unstable, self-reliance becomes invaluable. Throughout this series, *The Backyard Renaissance*, I will share with you the lost skills of self-sufficiency and healthy living. Come with me and other do-it-yourself experimenters, and rediscover the joys and successes of simple self-reliance.

Copyright © 2016 by Caleb Warnock and Logan J. Lyons

Published by Familius LLC, www.familius.com

Familius books are available at special discounts for bulk purchases for sales promotions or for family or corporate use. Special editions, including personalized covers, excerpts of existing books, or books with corporate logos, can be created in large quantities for special needs. For more information, contact Premium Sales at 559-876-2170 or email specialmarkets@familius.com.

Library of Congress Catalog-in-Publication Data
2016961879
ISBN 9781944822552

Edited by Maggie Wickes
Cover design by David Miles
Book design by David Miles and Maggie Wickes

10 9 8 7 6 5 4 3 2 1
First Edition

CONTENTS

WELCOME TO SUCCESSFUL GARDENING IN UTAH!

W hat stops you from loving your garden?

Weeds, bugs, water bills, struggling plants, stunted harvests, expensive "fixes"— these are the things that stop many people from growing more of their own food.

Gardening in Utah is unlike gardening almost anywhere else. We face unique challenges, but there are simple solutions that can turn your garden from a weed-infested burden to a source of health, food, and joy. If your garden feels like a burden, you are not likely to keep it up. On top of which, you are not likely to teach your children the skills they will need to love growing their own food. My goal in writing this book is to make stress-free, weed-free gardens filled with delicious food possible for everyone who is interested in learning how.

The advice in most gardening books—written by authors who have never grown anything in the high desert climate of the Rocky Mountain West—is unusable here. Let's examine, one by one, the unique challenges that can derail any Utah garden if you don't know the tips and tricks needed for success here. This book will give you specific solutions for every unique growing challenge in our beautiful desert state.

PROBLEMS AND SOLUTIONS

LACK OF SUMMER RAIN

Utah's prime gardening season (days with no frost) is June, July, and August. The problem is that Utah can get, on average, less than an inch of rain in each of these months. The typical vegetable garden must have between 1 and 1.5 inches of water per week.

What little rain does fall is made fairly useless because of two things:

First, the soil is baked so dry in these months that when rain does fall, it rarely penetrates the soil. Most summer rainstorms last ten minutes or less, and rain falls heavily, which can give people the false impression that it's a "good" summer rain. But by digging down a couple of inches, it is clear that the rain has failed to penetrate. The top inch or two are damp, and the soil below that is bone dry (especially in areas not watered with a sprinkling system).

Second, the extreme heat causes whatever moisture is near the top of the soil to evaporate quickly. Without this consistent moisture, it is nearly impossible for seeds to germinate. Most seeds must be planted near the top of the soil, yet this is the part of the soil that is most difficult to keep wet. If a gardener can get the seeds moist, they will germinate—but if the soil is then allowed to dry out, the seedling can die even before it produces its first leaf.

THE SOLUTION: The settlers and pioneers who turned this

UTAH AVERAGE PRECIPITATION

JAN: 1.25 INCHES   JUL: 0.61 INCHES

FEB: 1.25 INCHES   AUG: 0.69 INCHES

MAR: 1.79 INCHES   SEP: 1.21 INCHES

APR: 1.99 INCHES   OCT: 1.52 INCHES

MAY: 1.95 INCHES   NOV: 1.45 INCHES

JUN: 0.98 INCHES   DEC: 1.41 INCHES

SOURCE: http://www.wrh.noaa.gov/slc/climate/slcclimate/ SLC/pdfs/Highest%20and%20Lowest%20Precip.pdf state from an alkaline desert into a blooming garden watered once every seven to ten days, and their gardens thrived. For best success, we must design a garden that follows their watering schedule.

EXTREME OVERWATERING (PANTING PEPOS)

Because Utah's climate is so dry, most gardeners dramatically overcompensate by watering their garden way more than is healthy. This can cause many problems: tomatoes, watermelons, and cantaloupes split; nutrients are washed out of the soil, causing leaves to turn yellow; and the overwatered soil becomes more alkaline. All of this stunts the growth of plants, which forces the gardener to use petrochemical fertilizers to keep the plants healthy. In effect, this is the equivalent of hydroponic gardening, which means you are growing plants in water instead of soil. When you add up the costs of water (which is increasingly expensive), seeds, and fertilizer, many gardeners find that the vegetables are cheaper at the store.

THE SOLUTION: Create a garden designed for low water use in the desert.

INSECT OASIS INFESTATION

The worst problem caused by overwatering is that a garden can become an oasis for pests. A common gardening question people have is:

"I have X pest killing X plant in my garden. What do I do?"

The solution comes in how often the garden is being watered. Many Utah gardeners are watering their gardens three times a week, and that's why they have pests. Any garden that is overwatered becomes an oasis in the desert for every pest imaginable. As long as overwatering continues, the pests will remain.

THE SOLUTION: Create a garden designed for low water use in the desert.

LACK OF SUMMER HUMIDITY

Because Utah air is so dry, plants and soil dry out much faster than they do in areas with humidity. The hanging baskets of flowers sold in every nursery and big box store in early summer are the best example of this problem. A vegetable or flower planted in the ground can lose water from only the top of the soil. A plant in a pot, however, evaporates moisture on the top, sides, and bottom. Because of this, potted plants struggle in the desert. The lack of humidity means the air is so dry that it literally sucks moisture from pots. Pots have to be watered almost daily just to keep them alive, or you have to use expensive chemical soil additives and watering systems. Basically that means more time spent babysitting a pot and trying to fight Mother Nature. Instead of fighting, gardeners who find success in Utah are those who design all aspects of their garden to work hand in hand with Mother Nature, not fight her.

THE SOLUTION: In Utah, you must garden down, not up. Many gardening books teach to plant seeds at the top of a furrow and plant potatoes and squash at the top of hills. In Utah, this is a big mistake, because your hill and furrow will simply drain water downward, making it harder and harder for your garden to access water. So, Utah gardeners should plant at the bottom of a furrow—the deeper, the better. Because of Utah's desert climate, when planting down, not up, you capture as much water as possible. In wet and humid climates, the goal is to drain water away from the roots because plants can suffer from too much water. In Utah, the struggle is getting enough water.

For pots and hanging gardens, it is best to use containers with no holes at the bottom. The goal is to keep water in the containers and not drain it away.

HIGH DAYTIME HEAT

This is a much bigger problem than most gardeners realize. Tomatoes are one of the worst victims. Tomato flowers will struggle to set any fruit above 85 degrees or below 70 degrees. Because of this, tomatoes struggle in Utah and often don't begin setting fruit in earnest until the temperatures begin to cool in early autumn. But Utah also often suffers from early and unpredictable frosts, meaning that just as the tomatoes begin to appear, the plants can be killed off. Many gardeners simply stop watering their tomatoes and give up on them entirely because they are so frustrated that the plants have not produced any fruit by mid-August. Others water them more and more, thinking this will solve the problem, but it only makes matters worse by encouraging soil disease and pests, which attack the plants that are already weakened by high heat. Many other plants *bolt* in the heat, meaning they stop developing fruit and instead begin to develop seed stalks. Most root vegetables (onions, carrots, parsnips, potatoes, etc.), greens such as lettuces, spinach, and many herbs, and brassicas (broccoli, kale, cabbages, brussels sprouts, and cauliflower) all struggle in heat.

THE SOLUTION: Lettuces, asparagus, stevia, and basils do much better in partial shade in Utah because it shields them from the worst of the heat. Onions, carrots, parsnips, potatoes, and brassicas all need to be planted much earlier than most people plant them. For example, I plant my carrot and parsnip seeds in February each year. The variety you plant also makes a huge difference. If you want tomatoes all summer, you need to plant Joe's Earliest Slicer or Winter Grape tomatoes,* for example. Many tomatoes are not suited for Utah's climate. Every single kind of seed that you plant should be a variety that is proven in your climate.**

*Available at SeedRenaissance.com.

**Go to SeedReanaissance.com for a full list of varieties best suited for Utah weather.

HIGH NIGHTTIME HEAT

Many people claim that tomatoes should have no problem setting fruit because the temperatures cool off at night. This is not true. In July and August, it is not unusual to have nighttime temps above 80 degrees, which does not allow for cooling off. High nighttime temperatures can also encourage more pests because they thrive in heat and are far less active when chilly. Pests will munch on the garden all night if the night is hot enough. Hot nights also dramatically increase plant stress and water evaporation.

THE SOLUTION: Grow only the vegetable varieties that are best suited for your environment.

ALKALINE SOIL

Vegetables and flowers thrive when the soil pH is neutral or slightly acidic. The soil in Utah is alkaline, which all by itself can stunt the growth of plants and cause smaller harvests.

THE SOLUTION: Use a design based on hugelkultur and compost.

ALKALINE WATER

While some Utah gardeners are aware their soil is alkaline, many forget that the water is also alkaline, and this doubles the trouble. Blueberries are the best example. Many gardeners want to grow blueberries, and they buy the plants, which come in specially treated soil. These soil treatments may last only a few weeks, or they may last the first year. Blueberries are just an extreme example.

THE SOLUTION: To counter the alkaline in the water, begin adding vinegar to the plants' water to acidify it (one teaspoon per cup of water). Making homemade fertilizer can also help this problem.

UNPREDICTABLE GROWING SEASON (FROST-FREE DAYS)

With Utah's mountains and valleys, it is hard to predict the growing season. Higher elevation generally means a shorter and more unpredictable growing season. Those who live in the mountains average only ninety-two frost-free days a year (a shockingly small growing season compared to most of the country). Snow in May and September is not rare. Spring can be three days instead of a month. Autumn is ideally long and pleasant, but it is not unusual for fall to be a week long, and then winter temperatures come hard. On top of the unpredictable season, weather from year to year can change drastically and make it hard for even experienced gardeners to cope.

THE SOLUTION: Utah gardeners should always use the short-est-season vegetables available and as many permaculture plants (perennial and self-seeding) as possible, because these will automatically adjust to the climate.

HEAVY CLAY SOIL (OR USELESS SANDY SOIL)

It has been said that Utah's clay soil is better for making dinner plates than for growing dinner. The clay is heavy and dense, which makes root vegetables struggle and also harbors disease. More importantly, clay soil is the worst for starting seeds. Seeds prefer friable, slightly acidic soil. To make matters worse, no matter how much organic matter you till or layer into your soil, natural enzymes often change that organic matter to clay soil within two to three years. This can be especially frustrating for inexperienced gardeners who pay big money and spend a lot of time amending their soil only to see all that amendment quickly turned to clay. If you are not sure if your soil is clay or sand or humus, dig a hole the size of a drinking cup and pour a cup of water in the hole. If the water is still in the hole ninety seconds later, your soil is heavy clay. If the water vanishes in less than thirty seconds, your soil is sandy. Sandy soil appears in pockets in Utah, especially near gravel deposits, and drains water so fast that it can be very difficult to grow anything.

THE SOLUTION: Whether your soil is clay or sand, the solution is in choosing the right design for your Utah garden.

EXTREMELY STONY SOIL

Not only is most of our soil clay, but most of it is also marred with stones. Stones cause root vegetables like carrots and parsnips to become deformed and smaller than they should be. All root vegetables struggle in stony soil. Even planting peas and squash seeds can be hard in soil that is filled with stones, and roots have to work extra hard to find their way to a good hold.

THE SOLUTION: It's all in the design. This book will show you a design to solve this problem and more, with some alternatives to help those in specific situations.

RHIZOMATOUS WEEDS

One of Mother Nature's peculiar adaptations for the desert climate is the rhizomatous weed. A rhizome is a specialized underground stem that allows weeds to "plant" themselves by spreading aggressively underground. The worst of these in Utah is quackgrass. Once your property is infested with quackgrass, it is nearly impossible to get rid of. You can knock it back with chemicals, but because it spreads underground, it just keeps coming back, over and over. Quackgrass can infest entire properties, and there is nothing you can do to remove it from the soil.

THE SOLUTION: Abandon the soil and start new.

WEED SEED BANK

Weeds are not going anywhere. Studies have shown that there

is a fifty-year "bank" of field bindweed (also called morning glory) in the soil. This means that even if you managed to control your bindweed so that another seed never fell on your garden, bindweed would still grow for another fifty years because of seeds stored in the soil. Mother Nature has ingeniously invented a way to control and store seeds so that they will grow over decades instead of all growing the year after they are dropped by the mother plant. This genius, however, is a Utah gardener's downfall. Mother Nature is smarter. No matter the amount of chemicals poured on the soil, the bindweed will never go away.

THE SOLUTION: As with rhizomatous weeds—abandon the soil.

LOW NATURAL WATER TABLE AND *SOIL OCEAN*

In climates where it actually rains, the water table can be near the surface of the garden, which is another reason that most garden books say to plant "up" in hills and at the top of furrows to encourage drainage. Not in Utah! The water table in Utah is low, and state officials have said the water table is actually dropping each year. All of this means that garden soil actually drains water away faster and faster.

I call this phenomenon the *soil ocean*. For anything to live in the wild, there has to be a reserve of water (an ocean) contained inside the soil. You can find this ocean in your backyard by taking a shovel and digging down until you find soil that is damp. This is often easy to do in yards that have sprinkler systems, but you have to remember that this kind of soil ocean is artificial and temporary—it exists only because you are creating artificial rain (an artificial microclimate) with your sprinkler system. If you go to any wild space or blank lot, you will have to dig much deeper to find soil that contains any amount of moisture, especially in July and August.

You might be asking yourself why this matters if you have a hose or a sprinkler system. Is it relevant to you? Yes, because all the water that everyone uses in the garden immediately begins to head toward this soil ocean. This is why Utah gardens dry out so fast—because all the water you sprinkle onto your grass and garden moves downward through the soil and does not stop until it reaches the soil ocean. If your garden is not carefully designed, you can waste huge amounts of water trying to keep your garden happy because all your water is simply draining away.

THE SOLUTION: It lies in the design of your garden.

EGYPTIAN COMPOST PRODUCTION

The entire reason that Egypt is famous today is because of the tombs and mummies found there over the years. In normal circumstances, a human body would have quickly turned to compost, but in Ancient Egypt, the climate was so dry that even bodies buried four thousand years ago are still found intact in tombs—rare indeed. Utah has a similar problem. Because Utah's climate lacks both rain and humidity, composting is slow at best. The rest of the country uses compost piles (or compost bins or rotating barrels, if you want to produce only tiny amounts), but in Utah, those methods can take years to make compost.

THE SOLUTION: Use a pit to make composting fast and easy without turning. This solution is beyond the scope of this book, but you can get all the details in my book *Shallow-Pit Garden Composting*.

OVER-FERTILIZING

For a garden to thrive, plants must have nitrogen. Utah's soil is a little low on potassium and phosphorus, but is extremely lacking when it comes to natural nitrogen. This is why sales of fertilizer boom in Utah, for both lawns and gardens. The problem is that gardeners try to fertilize their garden like they fertilize their lawns—using way too much. Lawns are deceptive because you can over-fertilize all you want and the lawn does not suffer.

Gardens are different than lawns. If you over-fertilize the lawn, it just turns an unnatural shade of jewel green. If you put too much fertilizer on a garden, the plants also turn that weird green color, and they grow huge, but they don't produce much food because nitrogen overstimulates the growth of leaves at the expense of the fruit. For example, summer squash and tomatoes grow huge plants if you put too much nitrogen in the soil but produce far fewer zucchinis and tomatoes. The result is a garden that looks lush but produces little to eat. This also happens with some flowers. Cosmos flowers are the most susceptible. They will grow huge plants with few flowers if they are fertilized much at all. In our zeal to produce the perfect garden, we actually cost ourselves the ultimate prize—the food.

THE SOLUTION: Garden organically without ever purchasing any commercial fertilizer.

SOLUTIONS FOR SUCCESSFUL GARDENING IN UTAH

DESIGN

garden that is not designed correctly—and specifically—for Utah will never thrive.

In Utah, correct design can give you a garden which:

- is permanently 95 percent weed-free.
- is organic and produces more than your garden ever did using commercial fertilizer.
- thrives on benign neglect, meaning the garden needs little or no babysitting. The garden should just grow food

for you without ruling your life or commandeering all your free time.

- causes no harm. You should never have to worry that you have poisoned your children's long-term health with pesticides, herbicides, and chemicals.
- requires no tilling. You don't till the garden, because tilling harms the natural fertility of the soil. Explaining this is beyond the scope of this book, but you can read all about it in my *No-Till Gardening* book.
- requires little water, needing water once a week at the most and once every two to three weeks ideally.
- is self-seeding and perennial. The majority of the garden plants itself. (To learn more about this, read *Creating a Permaculture Food Forest* and the chapter on self-seeding garden plants in *More Forgotten Skills of Self-Sufficiency*.
- is bountiful. You really can be self-reliant. Your garden can feed your family without backbreaking work.

OPTION ONE: PERMANENT WEED-FREE GARDEN PATCH

This might seem crazy at first glance, but the benefits are enormous and long lasting. To create a garden that is permanently 95 percent weed-free, you simply remove the soil, line the garden, and fill it with tree shred and topped with compost.

Let me explain what I mean by 95 percent weed-free. Even if your compost is free of weed seeds (which are killed by high heat in the natural composting process), weed seeds will blow into your garden over time. Some weeds will sprout. I tell people to expect to do 5 percent of the weeding you used to, but you must invest this 5 percent of your weeding time wisely. It is okay for some weeds to sprout and grow, but you *must* commit to yourself that you will get rid of them before they get to seed. If you allow these few weeds to drop seeds on your clean garden compost, you will have a much larger weed problem the next year, and in a few years, you will have a weedy garden. Make sure all weeds are removed before they can drop seeds. If you commit to this, your garden will be easy to maintain for many years to come.

Let's go through that one step at a time.

STEP 1. Find the perfect location for your garden. Any spot with full sun is ideal.

STEP 2. Decide how large you want your garden to be. Think long term, and remember that you are likely to want a larger garden than you have now if your garden is weed-free and very low maintenance. People who use this weed-free design soon realize how easy gardening can be and often want a larger garden. It is cheaper and easier to make your garden large now than it is to expand later, so think carefully about how large you want your garden to be. Do you want a garden that is 10 feet by 10 feet? 25 by 25? 50 by 50? Consider your needs and constraints.

STEP 3. Remove 6 to 9 inches of topsoil. For most people, this means hiring someone with a small tractor to come in and scrape the soil away. CAUTION: Don't remove more than 9 inches of soil (except in a few instances we will discuss in a moment). Removing more than this makes the garden too deep, which requires extra water. This soil should be removed permanently because it will no longer be part of the garden. If your garden space is smaller, the topsoil can be removed with a shovel. If you can find a use for the discarded soil somewhere on your property, this is certainly cheaper than hiring someone to haul it away. I have used extra soil to create a small hill for the grandkids to play on, and I have used the soil as a berm for the north side of a geothermal greenhouse. It can also be scattered on pasture land or used as fill.

STEP 4. Once the topsoil is gone, line the hole where the soil has been removed with something that will hold water. Rolled plastic sheets of 4 mils or thicker works well. You could also use natural cotton fabric made waterproof with pine resin or beeswax, but it is not clear how long it might take for these naturally waterproof materials to break down in the soil, so you may have to re-line the garden after a few years if you use an all-natural material.

I GET A LOT OF QUESTIONS ABOUT WHETHER USING PLASTIC AS LINER IN THE GARDEN IS SAFE. PLASTIC IS STABLE AT MESOPHILIC TEMPERATURES, WHICH MEANS THAT ONCE IT IS COMPLETELY BURIED, IT SHOULD LAST DECADES IF NOT CENTURIES. THIS IS WHY PLASTIC WASTE IS SUCH A CONCERN. ONCE BURIED, IT STAYS AROUND FOR A LONG TIME. PLASTIC WILL QUICKLY BREAK DOWN IF EXPOSED TO DIRECT SUNLIGHT OR HIGH HEAT, BUT NEITHER OF THOSE WILL BE A WORRY UNDERGROUND.

STEP 5. On top of the plastic lining, fill the hole halfway with tree shred (available from any tree removal company) or natural tree mulch (sold at nurseries and home improvement stores). Remember that this will settle over time, so you want it to be as compact as possible. The size does not matter. You can use large pieces or small. You may not want to use whole branches because they can easily rip holes in the lining, which defeats the purpose. Be careful not to rip the lining when applying the shredded wood. Filling the hole halfway with wood shred is a principle of hugelkultur—a low-water gardening method which uses wood to capture and absorb water, releasing it to the roots of plants over time. This allows you to go up to three or four weeks without watering (depending on the month and other conditions).

STEP 6. Fill the rest of the hole with organic weed-free compost or composted manure—organic mushroom compost and well-composted horse manure are some examples. It is very important that the compost you use is free of weed seeds. If it is not, then the whole project is in vain. Remember that the compost will settle and filter down into the wood shred over the next several months, so you want to add enough now that it is heaping a couple inches higher than you intend it to end up. In other words, if you add 4 inches of compost on top of the tree shred, you may have only 2 inches of compost in a couple of months. If you intend to end up with 4 inches, add 6 inches now.

One final design note: If you choose this garden patch option, you can use stepping stones to create walking paths through the garden. It is always best to avoid walking where you intend to plant because compacting the soil inhibits the growth of plants. Make clear paths through the patch and stick to them.

A CAUTION ABOUT GARDENING IN COMPOST: COMPOST NEEDS TO CURE COMPLETELY BEFORE IT CAN BE USED OR IT WILL BE TOO "HOT," MEANING IT IS TOO NUTRIENT RICH. SEEDS WILL NOT GERMINATE, AND PLANTS WILL STRUGGLE. COMMERCIALLY PRODUCED COMPOST SOLD IN BULK MAY STILL BE HOT WHEN IT ARRIVES AT YOUR GARDEN, AND YOU MAY NOT KNOW THIS UNTIL YOU TRY TO PLANT A GARDEN AND NOTHING GROWS. IF YOUR COMPOST IS HOT, IT MEANS IT HAS NOT FINISHED THE COMPOSTING PROCESS. IT MAY TAKE SEVERAL MONTHS OR A YEAR BEFORE THE COMPOST HAS "COOLED" ENOUGH TO BE USABLE. IF YOUR COMPOST IS HOT, YOU MAY HAVE TO FORGO A SUMMER GARDEN AND PLANT AN AUTUMN GARDEN INSTEAD. HOWEVER, THE WAIT WILL BE WORTH IT FOR A GARDEN THAT IS 95 PERCENT WEED-FREE!

The benefits of this option: You have a garden space that is permanently 95 percent weed-free because it uses no soil and uses much less water because of the waterproof lining and wood shred which absorbs and stores the water. The garden is at the natural soil level, not above the ground, so it uses less water because it drains less.

OPTION TWO: PERMANENT WEED-FREE GARDEN BEDS

The only difference between Option One and Option Two is that instead of doing a large garden patch, you choose to remove the soil only in smaller beds, leaving the native soil for your pathways between your beds. If you choose this option, here are some things to consider:

- In this option, you will only remove the topsoil where you want the growing beds to be. The pathways will be left as native soil. The beds should be lined and filled as described in Option One.

- Do not create growing beds that are wider than you can easily reach, because any part of the bed that you cannot easily reach will become wasted space and a haven for weeds. No more than 3 feet wide is recommended. The beds can be as long as you want.

- You will still need to manage the weeds on the paths. The best way to do this is to line the paths with weed fabric or plastic sheeting and then cover this with a thick layer (at least 4 inches) of tree shred to protect the lining and shade weeds that will sprout below the lining.

The benefits of this option: You have to do less excavation of the native soil, and it requires less compost. The garden is permanently 95 percent weed-free because it uses no soil and uses much less water because of the waterproof lining and wood shred which absorbs and stores the water. The garden is at the natural soil level, not above the ground, so it uses less water because it drains less.

OPTION THREE: ABOVE-GROUND GARDEN BOXES

In this option, you don't dig down at all, and you don't remove any topsoil. Instead, you use wood or other materials to create garden boxes that sit on the ground. The taller these boxes are, the more water they will need because of drainage. Make the boxes as low to the ground as possible, preferably 4 inches tall or less. Instead of lining the box with flat waterproof lining, create a partial "cup" in the box by using the lining to come up the side of the box halfway. This creates a waterproof bowl or cup in the bottom half of the box to hold the water where the wood shred can absorb it. The box should be lined only in the bottom half, because in spring (after the snow melts), you will have a pool of water if you don't have some drainage, and drainage could again become a problem in autumn or if you have an unusually rainy summer. This way, once the "cup" or "bowl" in the bottom half of the box has fill, the water will naturally spill over the sides of the lining, so the box has some drainage. The pathways around the boxes should be lined and covered with mulch as described in Option Two.

Design note: This option will use more water because it is entirely above the ground, which means that the sides of the box will be heated by the sun, causing more evaporation than in Option One or Two. The benefit of this design is that no excavation of soil is required

OPTION FOUR: AT-HEIGHT GARDEN BOXES

Because of physical limitations, some people cannot bend down to garden at ground level. Custom-built garden boxes can be created in several ways. Costco sells a heavy-duty professional-grade black plastic box for $9 at this writing which I use for my greenhouses. This makes a great raised garden box. The boxes are also designed by the manufacturer to securely stack (and they come with heavy-duty lids) so you can stack two or three to garden at your preferred height. The bottom boxes can be filled with water for stability and thermal mass (this water should be drained before winter so ice doesn't warp or crack the boxes). This is likely to be the cheapest, easiest long-term solution to gardening at height. You can also have boxes custom-made for you, but if you have a box that is 3 feet tall, for example, you don't want the water to be able to drain down 3 feet, or it will be very difficult to keep the plants watered. Instead, fill the lower space with fill dirt or other material and then use a liner or boxes or other containers to create a bowl or cup in the upper portion of the box so that the water is contained near the top. This will greatly reduce the amount of water you will need. However, no matter what you do, this method will require the most water because so much surface area is exposed to heat and thus evaporation. Fill the bottom half of your container or "bowl" with wood shred and the top half with weed-free compost. Home improvement and garden stores often sell bags of clean, weed-free clay. You will need to water less if you mix this clay with the compost in the top of your at-height garden boxes because the clay will help hold the water in the compost as much as possible.

EXCEPTIONS:

- Potatoes cannot be grown in hugelkultur gardens (such as the garden designs described in the book). See *Forgotten Skills of Self-Sufficiency Used by the Mormon*

Pioneers for tips on how to grow potatoes in straw instead of soil.

- Long-type carrots cannot be grown in garden beds with tree shred. You will need to grow Danvers carrots, which are short stumpy carrots that are only about 4 inches long, or Paris Market carrots*, which grow at the top of the soil.

*Both are available at SeedRenaissance.com.

- Parsnips, salsify, and carrot-type radishes (any root vegetable with a long underground root) cannot be grown in hugelkultur gardens. To grow these, you will need to reserve a section of your new garden (created using the designs listed in this book) that is 9 inches deep with just compost and no tree shred. This can be a small portion of the garden, but it must be large enough to rotate root vegetables over the years. You can also grow potatoes in this section of the garden.
- Raspberries and goji berries can be grown in the designs listed in this book because they are shallow-rooted, but blackberries, currants, and other deep-root berries will need to be in the section of garden that is 9 inches of compost with no tree shred.
- Orchard trees cannot be grown in the designs listed

here. Instead, you can line the ground surrounding orchard trees with weed fabric covered with 6 inches of wood shred to discourage weeds. However, if you have rhizomatous quackgrass in your orchard, it will likely grow through the weed fabric and wood chips, so you will need to line the orchard with sheet plastic that is 4 mils thick or thicker and then cover this with at least 6 inches of tree shred to protect it from heat and sun. This will keep your orchard free of weeds.

CALEB'S RECIPES FOR FREE, HOMEMADE FERTILIZER

COMPOST TEA:

STEP 1. Fill any size of bucket one-third full with compost. This should be finished compost, meaning whatever it started out as, it has now all turned into rich black soil (or brown, in the case of mushroom compost). It should be cool to the touch, not hot. Hot compost is still breaking down. This compost can be of your own making or purchased.

STEP 2. Fill the rest of the bucket with water. Leave this outside to sit in a sunny place for three sunny days. You are essentially making sun tea out of compost. If you don't have three sunny days, wait until you have a total of three sunny days, or one week, whichever comes first.

STEP 3. Stir the compost tea, preferably with something disposable, like a stick. Get two more buckets roughly the same size as you are using for the tea. Pour one-third of the tea into each bucket. You now have three buckets, each one-third full with the ripe tea.

STEP 4. Fill each of the buckets with water. This step is essential. Compost tea that is not diluted can be too "hot" which means it is too rich in nutrients and can damage your plants. By filling your buckets with water, you have just diluted the tea using a two-to-one ratio: one part compost tea, two parts water.

STEP 5. Use the diluted tea to water your garden. You can pour it into a garden watering can, or you can just take the bucket and pour it over the plants you want to water. Be careful that you don't get the tea on yourself—the tea will stain clothes and shoes, and it does have an odor.

GREEN LEAF FERTILIZER TEA

If you find that compost is in short supply, use this recipe. Please keep in mind that this fertilizer has a stronger odor than compost tea. If you have a small property with close neighbors that might be offended by the smell for a couple days, this might not be the recipe for you. You can use the compost tea recipe.

STEP 1. Fill any size of bucket one-third full of green leaves of any kind. These can be weeds from the garden, the outer leaves of vegetable plants (like the outer lettuce leaves you would probably not use anyway), vegetables (leaves and bulbs) that have been munched on by the chickens, the rabbit, a caterpillar, grasshoppers, leaves from trees (fresh, not dried), chemical-free grass clippings, anything green, etc. If you are using weeds, do not include weeds that have seeds on them. Weeds in flowers are fine. The roots are fine. Dirt on the roots is fine. You can use all the same kind of leaves or a mixture of any kind of leaves. You can break open the base-ball bat zucchinis and add them in, or tomatoes that were touching the ground and have begun to rot—anything from the garden that is vegetative and alive.

STEP 2. Fill the rest of the bucket with water. Leave this outside to sit in a sunny place for three sunny days. You are essentially making sun tea out of green leaves. If you don't have three sunny days, wait until you have a total of three sunny days, or one week, whichever comes first.

STEP 3. When the tea is ripe, carefully pour the water out

of the bucket into another bucket, leaving behind the spent greens. The spent greens, which have now discolored, can be buried in the compost pit, compost pile, or hot bed. If you don't bury them, they will smell for several days.

STEP 4. Stir the leaf tea, preferably with something disposable, like a stick. Get two more buckets roughly the same size as you are using for the tea. Pour one-third of the tea into each bucket. You now have three buckets, each one-third full with the ripe tea.

STEP 5. Fill each of the buckets with water. This step is essential. Leaf tea that is not diluted can be too "hot" (meaning it is too rich in nutrients and can damage your plants). By filling your buckets with water, you have just diluted the tea using a two-to-one ratio: one part compost tea, two parts water. This makes it safe for your plants.

STEP 6. Use the diluted tea to water your garden. You can pour it into a garden watering can, or you can just take the bucket and pour it over the plants you want to water. Be careful that you don't get the tea on yourself—the tea will stain clothes and shoes, and it does have a strong odor. The odor disappears in a day or two, but not from the bucket. Rinse out the bucket with the hose, preferably over lawn grass, which can benefit from the residual nutrients.

Q & A

HOMEMADE FERTILIZER

Question: How much is a "dose" of this homemade fertilizer?

Answer: Enough to really soak the soil—as much as you would water if you were watering the garden with a watering can. There is no need for a precise measurement. You simply give the plants a good drink.

Question: Can I use my lawn grass clippings to make the fertilizer?

Answer: If you have not used any chemicals on your lawn grass. You don't want those same chemicals in your garden.

Question: Can I spray the tea on as foliar fertilizer (to be absorbed through the leaves)?

Answer: Yes, if you spray it straight. If you put it into one of those garden hose attachments, it's going to be too diluted. (Remember, you already diluted it once.) And if you try to put it in undiluted, it will stink and it won't be diluted to the right ratio. It is easier and faster to just water your plants with it.

Question: How soon after I use the fertilizer can I eat my vegetables?

Answer: Wash them, then eat them.

Question: How soon do I need to use the tea?

Answer: It can sit for several weeks if you like. It might develop a harmless white mold on the top, which you can skim off with a stick and throw out. The smell will get stronger. Your neighbors might glare at you. Definitely don't let the kids or the dog accidentally tip it over onto them—they will stink to high heaven, even after you wash them with soap.

Question: Can I bottle it up to save for later?

Answer: It is not recommended, but if you really want to, store only the diluted tea. Never store the undiluted tea because it might develop gases and explode out of your container. Never store in the sun or heat for the same reason. Your best bet is just to not store it, or if you want to store it, don't store it for very long or in any place where you will mind if it leaks or explodes and stinks. Don't store in glass jars.

Question: Can I put a lid on the bucket in case it smells or cover the bucket in some other way?

Answer: No, especially not if you are making the Green Leaf Tea. A closed container is very likely to explode, kind of like making homemade root beer that is too happy. You might be able to cover the bucket to make compost tea, but I have never tried it with a lid, so you will be experimenting.

Question: How do you rotate your carrots and potatoes if they have to stay in just your tall raised beds?

Answer: Rotating where you plant your vegetables each year helps reduce disease in the garden. Gardens should be rotated on a four-year-schedule or longer, meaning you don't plant the same type of vegetable in the same spot for at least four years. When my straw potatoes are done, I move the straw to the compost pit. Then I fill the potato bed up so I can now use it to grow carrots, filling the bed with a new mix of half compost and half sand, using compost I make on my own property. To rotate my potatoes into my former carrot bed, I remove the top two-thirds of the compost and use it to top off other beds or to top off new beds. I plant my potatoes in the bottom third of the compost that is left and then fill the rest with straw. Especially with potatoes, it is essential to rotate them every year so you don't encourage disease to build up in the soil—and it will, if you don't rotate.

WATERING YOUR GARDEN

Use a single overhead oscillating sprinkler. You may need to raise it up to make sure that it gets over the corn and every other tall vegetable as the summer goes on. Then water about once every eight to ten days overnight—a good, deep watering.

Question: What about using drip lines? I know lots of people who use drip lines.

Answer: I do not recommend drip lines ever. Drip lines can clog so easily—even the new supposedly less cloggy kind— and they cost hundreds of dollars to install.

Question: My garden won't make it ten days without water. It will die.

Answer: That shouldn't be the case, with two exceptions: First, if your raised beds are tall, you are going to have to water more often. Second, if your temperature goes above 110-ish, you are going to need to water about every five days.

SEEDRENAISSANCE. COM GUIDE TO BASIC PLANTING IN THE ROCKY MOUNTAIN WEST

SEASONS

EARLY SPRING:

These vegetables can be planted outside as seed (not live plants) unprotected as soon as the soil can be worked in spring (usually in late January or early February). These vegetables depend on a long cold season for best performance. Carrots in particular do best when planted as early as possible. These will germinate slowly—some of these may come up quickly; some may take weeks. As soon as the ground has unfrozen and you can work the ground, you can plant these:

- **CARROTS**: Must have wet, cool soil without drying out for best germination. Carrots can be planted anytime in spring, but you will have the best germination if you plant them as soon as the soil can be worked, because they do not tolerate dry soil.

  Press seeds firmly into soil. Carrots seeds germinate best with sunlight and must be constantly moist, which is why we plant them so early. They don't mind cold and will withstand light freezes and several hard frosts as seedlings.

- **RUTABAGA**: Must have a long, cold period to produce a bulb, so they need to be planted as soon as possible. Spring is too late to plant these unless there is going to be a long, cold spring. These can be planted in late summer for early winter harvest, but they may or may not produce a large bulb.

  Lightly rake seeds into the soil, just barely covering. Press soil firmly. Keep moist, which is why we plant them so early. Rutabaga hates hot days and will never produce a bulb without a long, cool period so it is essential to plant these seeds the moment the ground can be worked in spring. Very cold tolerant.

- **BROAD WINDSOR FAVA BEANS:** These flower in the snow and need cold soil. These can also be planted in early fall.

    Plant seeds 1 inch deep. Press soil firmly. This tall, skinny plant can be close together.

- **WINTER WHEAT:** Can also be planted anytime in the preceding fall before the ground freezes.

    Plant 1 inch deep, in rows 4–5 inches apart. Press soil firmly.

    Winter varieties, plant according to directions in my *Backyard Winter Gardening* book.

- **ONIONS:** Lightly rake seeds into soil and then press soil firmly.

- **GARLIC:** Can also be put out in the preceding autumn.

    Gently pull the garlic head into individual pieces. Plant each clove so the root cap end of the clove is buried and the tip of the clove is at soil level. Space 4–5 inches apart. Press soil firmly.

SPRING:

These vegetables need to be planted as seed anytime in

spring (March, April). Keep in mind that the earlier you plant them, the less work you will have to do. It is very possible that vegetables planted in March as seed will never need to be watered until June or July. Plant the day before rain (or snow, if the ground is thawed) in the forecast.

- BRASSICAS: Cabbages, collard greens, kale, brussels sprouts, kohlrabi, cauliflower. They can be planted as live plants outside, without protection, beginning in late March. You will need to harden them off first. See notes below.

  Lightly rake seeds into soil and then press soil firmly and keep moist until germination. Once seedlings are up, thin as desired by removing "extra" seedlings. Cabbages, collards, and cauliflower will need 2 feet between plants. All others 12 inches.

- BEETS: Rake seeds into soil, press soil firmly, keep moist until germination.

- MANGELS: Rake seeds into soil, press soil firmly, keep moist until germination. Mangels (livestock fodder beets) ideally reach 20–30 pounds each and need good soil and 18 inches between plants.

- PERENNIALS: (flowers or vegetables) These can also be put out as live plants beginning in late March. For individual types, see SeedRenaissance.com for directions.

- **SUMMER WHEAT:** Plant 1 inch deep in rows 4–5 inches apart. Press soil firmly.
- **WINTER LETTUCE VARIETIES:** Can now be direct-seeded without a hot bed or protection. Lightly rake seeds into soil, press soil firmly.
- **ALL LETTUCE VARIETIES:** Can be seeded directly in the garden in mid-April. Lightly rake seeds into soil, press soil firmly.
- **ONION SEEDS, BULBS, AND ONION THREADS:** Can now go into the open garden.
- **PARSNIPS:** Rake seeds somewhat deeply into the soil, press soil firmly.
- **PEAS:** Plant 1 inch deep, press soil firmly.
- **POTATOES:** Plant in straw. Cut potatoes into small pieces with at least one eye. Lay the pieces 6 inches apart in a grid on the ground. Sprinkle generously with blood meal/bone meal if you are not using homemade fertilizers. Cover with 2–3 inches of compost, then 8–12 inches of straw. Water thoroughly.
- Remember that potatoes only grow up from where they are planted; they never grow down into the soil. Potatoes do not like heat. They love cool, well-drained medium. Straw growing is best and easiest.
- **ORACH:** Lightly rake seeds into soil, press soil firmly.

- **SPINACH**: Lightly rake seeds into soil, press soil firmly.
- **ALL ROOT VEGETABLES**: Lightly rake seeds into soil, press soil firmly.

AFTER ALL DANGER OF FROST:

These vegetables *cannot* be direct-seeded in the garden without protection until after the Average Last Frost Date (ALFD) in your area. The ALFD is not a guarantee; it is just the average last frost for your city. You can find your ALFD by typing the name of your city and "average last frost date" into Google. Nevertheless, you will still need to consult the ten-day weather report and keep an eye out for rogue frosts in the weather report. Tender seedlings will need to be carefully covered for protection, or they will need to be replanted if they die from frost kill. These include:

- **BEANS**: Plant 1/2 inch deep. Press soil firmly.
- **CORN**: Plant 1 inch deep. Press soil firmly.
- **CUCUMBERS**: Plant 1/2 inch deep. Press soil firmly.
- **FLOWERS**: (tender annuals) Lightly rake seed into soil. Press soil firmly.
- **MELONS, CANTALOUPE, WATERMELONS**: Plant 1/2 inch deep. Press soil firmly.
- **SQUASHES**: (pumpkins, summer squash, winter squash). Plant 1 inch deep. Press soil firmly.

- TOMATOES: Lightly rake seed into soil. Press soil firmly. Trials have shown that tomatoes direct-seeded give tomatoes before transplants every single time. It is essential that you use only the shortest day-count varieties possible, such as Stupice, Roma, and Snow Fairy.

HARDENING OFF: THIS MEANS TAKING LIVE PLANTS THAT HAVE BEEN RAISED IN A SHELTERED ENVIRONMENT (GREENHOUSE OR IN YOUR HOUSE) AND "HARDENING" THEM TO WITHSTAND THE DRAMATICALLY DIFFERENT ENVIRONMENT THEY WILL FACE OUTSIDE. THE OUTSIDE SOIL WILL BE COLDER AND THERE WILL BE WIND, DIRECT SUNLIGHT, TEMPERATURE SWINGS, PESTS, AND A DIFFERENT WATERING SYSTEM THAN THEY ARE USED TO. TO HARDEN OFF LIVE PLANTS, PUT THEM OUTSIDE DURING THE DAY FOR 2-3 DAYS THEN LEAVE THEM OUTSIDE OVERNIGHT AND SEE HOW THEY FARE. MAKE SURE THEY NEVER RUN OUT OF WATER. TRANSPLANT INTO THE OPEN GARDEN JUST BEFORE A RAINSTORM FOR BEST RESULTS. WATER THEM WELL. IF YOU HAVE PURCHASED TRANSPLANTS FROM A STORE, CHECK THEM VERY CAREFULLY FOR PESTS SUCH AS APHIDS BEFORE YOU INTRODUCE THEM TO YOUR GARDEN. IF THEY ARE INFESTED, THROW THEM AWAY.

PEPPERS: Lightly rake seed into soil. Press soil firmly.

AUTUMN GARDENING PLANTING:

These should be planted in late summer or early fall for harvesting in late autumn or early winter:

- **SALAD GREENS:** (mizuna, komatsuna, orach, spinach, mustard greens, etc.) Lightly rake seed into soil. Press soil firmly.
- **KALE:** Lightly rake seed into soil. Press soil firmly.
- **PEAS:** Plant 1/2 deep. Press soil firmly.
- **BROAD WINDSOR FAVA BEANS:** Must be planted in late summer to make beans in winter. Plant 1 inch deep.

   For winter growing options, see my *Backyard Winter Gardening* book.

DAY-COUNTS (ALSO CALLED DAYS TO MATURITY)

WHAT IS A DAY-COUNT?

A day-count is also called "days to maturity" and gives gardeners an idea of how long the season for a specific plant needs to be for it to successfully grow. Some cultivars (the fancy word for vegetable varieties) are ready to harvest earlier than others. For example, Brandywine and Cherry Roma tomatoes have a 90 day-count. Stupice has a 45 day-count. Stupice produces red, ripe tomatoes in half the time. (The vast majority of tomatoes have a 70+ day-count.)

1. If you plant late-maturity vegetable cultivars, you spend twice as much time waiting to harvest. If you had planted short day-counts (early-to-mature varieties), then you could have been eating fresh for a lot longer!

2. Short day-count plants are the best hedge against the weather. No one can predict whether there will be late frosts in spring or early frosts in the fall. Short day-count plants produce harvestable food as fast as possible.

3. If the goal is self-reliance, then getting food to the table is the highest goal, and the only way to get food to the table fastest is with the shortest day-count vegetables possible.

WHEN DOES THE DAY-COUNT START?

- For seeds, the day-count starts on the day that the plant's second set of leaves (called true leaves) are full size.
- For transplants, the day-count begins after the plant has been transplanted into the garden and the first new leaves since transplant are full size.

It is *essential* to notice that day-counts are much longer than the amount of time a plant spends in the garden. Both seeds and transplants will be in the garden for 3–4 weeks before their day-count can begin. So if you have an average 92-day growing season and you plant Brandywine tomatoes, which have a 90 day-count, you are not likely to harvest many of these tomatoes because you have a math problem:

> 30 days (approx) until day-count begins
> +90 day-count to harvest
> ———————————————
> 120 total days to harvest

If your average growing season is 92 days and the total days to harvest is 120 days, there is only a very small chance that you will have enough time for Brandywine tomatoes to ripen in your garden. You would have to bank on an unusually long growing season. To get a full harvest, you need to use the shortest day-count vegetables possible.

WHAT IS AVERAGE GROWING SEASON?

The Average Growing Season (AGS) is defined as the average number of frost-free days in your microclimate. As a general rule, the higher your altitude, the shorter your growing season. The AGS is calculated by the Extension Service using data collected by the National Weather Service. The best solution is to design your garden with the shortest day-count vegetables possible—and then, if the season turns out to be longer, then you will get a longer harvest as a bonus.

DETERMINATE VERSUS INDETERMINATE

 ome plants produce all their fruit at once and then die, and others keep steadily producing until the end of the growing season.

DETERMINATE: When the plant reaches its day-count, it bears a lot of fruit in a short window of time (about 3 weeks) and then dies.

INDETERMINATE: When the plant reaches its day-count, it bears fruit in a slow but steady stream until the plant is killed or made dormant by the end of season cold.

WHO DOES THIS AFFECT?

People who are canning or preserving food need determinate varieties. Whether you want determinate or indeterminate tomatoes (for example) depends on whether your goal is to have a few fresh ripe tomatoes every day or a whole bunch of ripe tomatoes at once so that you can bottle them for winter use. Another example: a determinate flower blooms for 3 weeks. An indeterminate flower produces continual blossoms beginning at the end of its day-count and going until the end of the season.

ARE ALL PLANTS EITHER DETERMINATE OR INDETERMINATE?

This is debated. At some level, the answer is yes. But in reality, only plants that produce food for preservation are labeled determinate or indeterminate. Tomatoes and berries are typically labeled this way, and sometimes melons, although melons can be tricky. Corn, for example, is always determinate—the whole crop is generally ripe in roughly 3 weeks, and once the corn has been harvested, no more corn is going to grow on that plant. Because of this, corn is not labeled "determinate" or "indeterminate" because it is always determinate and that is just "known." Tomatoes, however, might be determinate or indeterminate, which is why they are labeled by cultivar. Same thing with berries.

HOW DO YOU KNOW IF A PLANT IS DETERMINATE OR INDETERMINATE?

Consult your supply company or seed packet or see SeedRenaissance.com.

HOW TO WATER

MATURE PLANTS: every 8 to 10 days *in summer only*, overnight, with an overhead oscillating sprinkler. In spring, autumn, and winter, water only as needed, which will be rarely if ever.

SEEDS: In spring and autumn, seeds don't usually need to be watered if you plant them the day before a rainstorm. However, if the year is exceptionally dry, you may have to water occasionally, as needed. If a seedling has true leaves (the second set of leaves) and the soil is moist 1/2-inch deep, you don't need to water. In winter, water only as necessary in cold frames and greenhouses. When planting seeds *in summer only*, use the "plus one" method, which looks like this:

1   Plant the seeds and water.

2   Water the second day.

3   Skip watering for one day, water the second day.

4   Skip watering for two days, water on the third day.

5   Skip watering for three days, water on the fourth day, etc., until . . .

6   Skip watering for nine days, water on the tenth day. Now these seedlings can join the rest of the garden, which is watered roughly once every ten days.

Use common sense when it comes to watering. If temperatures are above normal, you may need to water more. If your garden gets a good rain, you will be able to water less. If the temperatures are lower than normal, you can water less. If the plants show signs of water stress, you need to water them. You can always check whether the garden needs water by digging down 2–3 inches and seeing if there is water in the garden bed. If the bed is dry 2–3 inches down, you need to water. Most garden plants require an inch of water per week. You can measure this by putting a cup or other contain in a garden pathway, turning on your water sprinkler, and turning it off when the container has accumulated at least an inch of water. However, if temperatures are above normal, you may need to water more. Infrequent, deep watering is much better for the garden (and lawn!) than watering several times a week. Keep an eye on your garden. I try to walk through my garden every day or two (if possible) to check it out. Remember that your reward for using less water will be far fewer garden pests and a lower water bill.

DOES ANY OF THIS APPLY TO SELF-SEEDING GARDEN PLANTS?

No. Self-seeding plants, as found at SeedRenaissance.com, will plant themselves and grow with nature. You don't need to do anything except provide them water with the rest of the garden in summer. In rare, rare circumstances it may be necessary to provide water to self-seeded seedlings in severe droughts in spring, but most of the time, spring is cool enough that even in droughts, these plants just grow longer roots and take care of themselves.

OTHER INFORMATION

Q&A FOR CALEB

Question: Caleb, do you spray your fruit trees?

Answer: No. We never have. We get enough unblemished fruit to be fine, and if we have to cut around some brown spots or wormholes, we do that—just like our grandparents did. Our garden and orchard is 100 percent organic, and we spray nothing, not even "organic" chemicals or oils.

Question: You say water my garden once every eight to ten days, but my garden is on the lawn watering system. What can I do?

Answer: You can move your lawn to a deep-drink watering schedule, as all water conservation experts recommend. Try deep watering once a week instead of three times a week. Or create a separate station on your system for your garden. Your lawn may develop a few brown spots. If parts of your lawn develop stress like this, water those parts by hand as needed, or adjust your sprinklers, or water a little more frequently. I'm a big believer that we don't need to have "perfect" lawns in the middle of the desert. However, not all my clients agree with me on this. For some people, their lawn is their showpiece.

Question: How do I save seed from my garden?

Answer: I teach seed-saving classes every year, and the online class is available at SeedRenaisssance.com.

Question: What kind of tomato cages do you use?

Answer: The cheap ones. I grow my tomato plants close together, and then I slightly bend the cages toward each other so they "lean" on each other and support each other.

ABOUT THE AUTHOR

aleb Warnock is the popular author of eighteen books, including *Forgotten Skills of Self-Sufficiency Used by the Mormon Pioneers, The Art of Baking with Natural Yeast, Backyard Winter Gardening for All Climates, More Forgotten Skills*, and the Backyard Renaissance Collection. He is the owner of SeedRenaissance.com, where you can sign up for his email newsletters. Find his Youtube channel at http://bit.ly/1OevHxT

ABOUT FAMILIUS

Welcome to a place where mothers are celebrated, not compared. Where heart is at the center of our families, and family at the center of our homes. Where boo boos are still kissed, cake beaters are still licked, and mistakes are still okay. Welcome to a place where books—and family—are beautiful. Familius: a book publisher dedicated to helping families be happy.

VISIT OUR WEBSITE: WWW.FAMILIUS.COM

Our website is a different kind of place. Get inspired, read articles, discover books, watch videos, connect with our family experts, download books and apps and audiobooks, and along the way, discover how values and happy family life go together.

JOIN OUR FAMILY

There are lots of ways to connect with us! Subscribe to our newsletters at www.familius.com to receive uplifting daily inspiration, essays from our Pater Familius, a free ebook every month, and the first word on special discounts and Familius news.

BECOME AN EXPERT

Familius authors and other established writers interested in helping families be happy are invited to join our family and contribute online content. If you have something important to say on the family, join our expert community by applying at:

www.familius.com/apply-to-become-a-familius-expert

THE MOST IMPORTANT WORK

YOU EVER DO WILL BE

WITHIN THE WALLS OF YOUR

OWN HOME.

CPSIA information can be obtained
at www.ICGtesting.com
Printed in the USA
LVOW10s2124221216
518169LV00001B/3/P